箪笥から鍔の写真

＋鍔 はがき

大阪市淀川区大阪

Yodogawa-Ku, Osaka Prefecture

At the bottom of an iron bound chest (*Tansu*) under a pile of documents, some old photos were found. The photos may have been a record of a tsuba collection pieced together over many years, preserved and treasured by the collector.

As many of us will find, those to whom we leave our treasures may not value them as we did. What became of the tsuba? We may never know, but as a legacy to this anonymous collector, I have compiled this work to the best of my ability to preserve at least the images of his collection. I hope I have done it some justice.

The photos were taken November 1975

(The contents from the Tansu purchased on-line from a Japanese auction site Feb. 2014.)

© 2020 by the author of this book. The author retains sole copyright to his contributions to this book.

"Those to whom we leave our
treasures may not value them
as we did."

我々がしたように、我々の宝物
を残して誰にそれらはそれらを
大切にしないかもしれない

D.R.R.

Photos from the Tansu

Cloud Dragon, Ryū -no-Kumo 雲の龍

Monk & Child with balance toy (Omote オモテ)

Dozing Child 居眠りお子様 (Ura 裏面) kinko

Sukashi, Ginger & birds Daisho (Katana 刀)

Sukashi, Ginger & birds Daisho (Wakizashi 脇差)

Sukashi, Horse, Uma 馬 *(Omote オモテ)*

Sukashi, Horse, Uma 馬 *(Ura 裏面)*

Uma 馬 *(Horse) Katana* 刀

Uma 馬 *(Horse) Wakizashi* 脇差

Bamboo and Wild Pheasants 野生のキジ

Kaneiye Style, Fune 船. *A boat*

Kan-mimi, plugged hitsu-ana (ume 埋)

Kan-mimi, Scrolls and Lotus, with Inome (boar's eyes)

Kamakura style 鎌倉. *Five tier temple,* 5層の神殿

Fuchidori style ふちどり *sukashi.* 千鳥の家紋

Yoshiro-zogan, Butterfly and blossom sukashi

Sukashi-kaku (squared openings) with stylized landscape

Heianjo 平安城 *Square, Foliate design*

Heianjo 平安城, *Inome (boar's eyes)*

Long eared Rabbits or Sedge hats, Kin-zogan
ウサギの耳あるいはスゲの帽子。象眼金

Sea Cucumbers and pine needles ナマコと松葉

Catfish ナマズ- sukashi Tsuchime-ji (hammered finish)

Shoami, Kumo (Clouds) 雲- sukashi

Buddhist mandala 仏教の曼荼羅 *Iroe, kinko*

Daikon 大根 *, White Radish, Ten-zogan*

Sage on a Donkey ロバに乗って司祭 , *katakiribori carving*

Cloud Dragon, Kumo no ryū 雲の龍 , *kinko*

Wild Goat 野生ヤギ

Rat and family banner ラット及び家紋

(Nanako ground) Family crest flowers 矢車の花

Flowering vines and Chiku no Koto 琴、花やつる *, kinko*

Bundles of Noshi 熨斗*, sukashi, gold Ategane*

Sea cucumber & Daisies, ナマコとのヒナギク *with Fukurin*

Apple 林檎 *Ko-sukashi with Fukurin*

Golden clouds 黄金の雲 *Sukashi*

Shinchi-zogan の真鍮象嵌 *(brass inlay)*

Budo 葡萄. *Grape, Kawari-gata Hitsu-ana*

Heianjo school (Kyoto) Frost on the grass 草の上に霜

Family crest 家紋図鍔 *(kamon) Raimon, Migaki Ji* (磨地)

Tsuchime-ji finish, Octagon 八角形, single udenuki-ana

Buddist Wheel of life, Attributed to Yamakichibei 山吉兵

Nobuiye, Myochin 明珍 *, Honeycomb/Tortoiseshell*

Hôô 鳳凰 *A Phoenix with Kiri flower, dote-mimi*

Large lobed Mokko

Elongated Mokko, Amida Yasuri design

Wheel, attributed to Kachushi school

Dote-mimi sukashi, Garden knife and daikon 大根 *(radish)*

Mokko Nightshade

Waves (Nami) and droplets

Star Chrysanthemum and flowers (Nanako ground)

Nanban Dragons, unusual shaped hitsu-ana

Yokoya School, Katakiri, Shishi (temple Lion)

Miochin style, Tsuchime, Mokume (wood knot) design

Baika 梅花. *Plum Blossom. Zogan and katakiribori carving*

Usagi-zu (rabbit) under the moon, Iroe, in raised relief.

Kyo-sukashi, Spindle and diamond flowers 主軸とダイヤモンドの花

Carved in the round, Nikubori-ji-sukashi 牡丹 Botan. Peony

Owari ,Tomoe, diamond and birds 巴、ダイヤモンド、野鳥

Sukashi, interlocking circles and droplets Yama-gata hitsu-ana

Gomoko-zogan, Boars eyes & Kiri mon, Ji-sukashi

Ko-Shoami school, Sukashi Kiri Mon

Shoami school, Shinchi-zogan, plants with Ten-zogan

Onin school 応仁 *Ten-zogan*テン象嵌

Sukashi, multi Sekigane with Ategane filled hitsu-ana

Ko-Shoami style, Yo-Sukashi (gourd ladles) heavy Tagane-ato

Chidori **チドリ** *Plover bird, Miochin style*

Hiashi-Yasurime-zu

Kyo Kenjyo, gold overlay (Nunome) 京、金象嵌

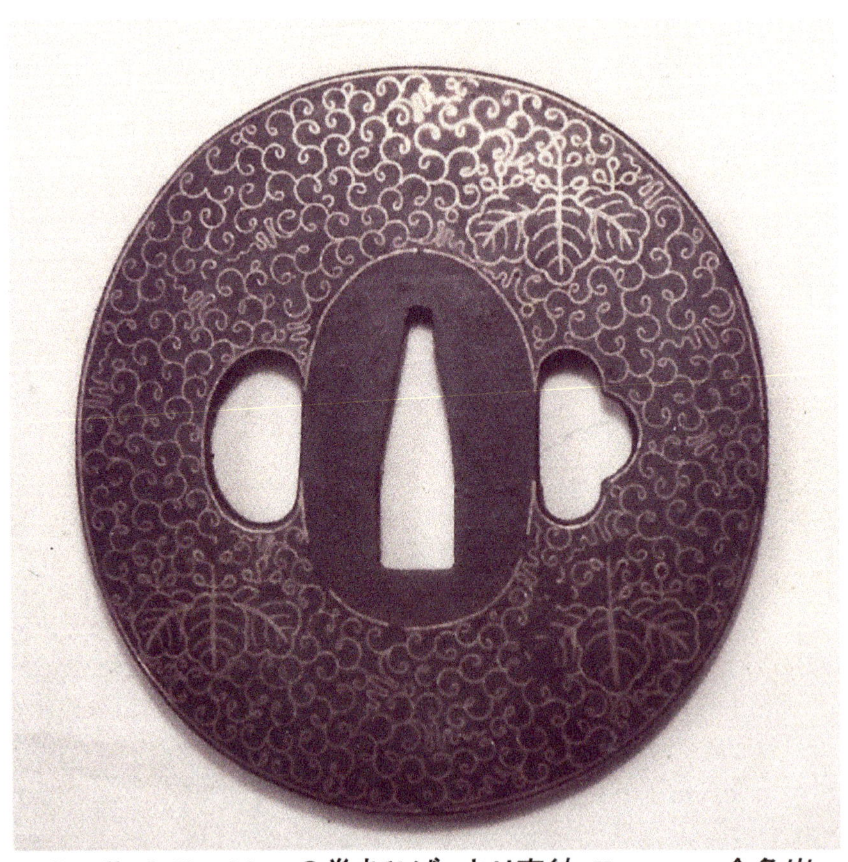

Scrolls & Kiri Mon の巻きひげ、キリ家紋, *Kin-zogan* 金象嵌

USED TERMS

AMIDA YASURI (file marks radiating from the centre of the tsuba plate that resemble the halo of the Amida (Buddha).

ATEGANE 当金 (metal plug in the Kozuka or Kogai-ana)(soft metal insets in sukashi)(see: UME)

CHIKU-NO-KOTO (thirteen string, musical instrument like a harp)

DAIKON 大根 (A Japanese white radish)

DAISHO (combining form Daitō large + Shotō short sword , Pair of swords Katana & Wakizashi , also matched tsuba as a pair)

FUKURIN 覆輪 (rim cover of a tsuba often different metal to main body)

GOMOKU-ZOGAN (dirt inlay, scrap inlay)

HIASHI-YASURIME-ZU (lines radiating from centre, starburst)

HITSU-ANA (opening/s at the side of Nakago-ana for Kogai & or Kozuka in tsuba)

INOME (lit. eye of a wild boar) (heart shaped opening in sukashi)

IROE (colouring, lit. Coloured picture)

ITO-SUKASHI 地透 (thin line piercing/ opening design on tsuba)

KAMON 家 (family crest)

KATANA 刀 (larger of the two swords, usually worn by Samurai)

KATAKIRI-BORI (carving at an acute angle, one side of the cut is low while other is near vertical)

KATCHUSHI TSUBA (made by armour maker)

KEBORI 毛彫 ('hair carving' very fine carved lines)

KIKU (Chrysanthemum)

KINKO (general term for soft metal)

KIRI 桐 (Paulownia tree/ flower)

KOGAI-HITSU-ANA (an opening for Kogai in tsuba)

KO-SUKASHI (small element removed as design)

KOZUKA-ANA (an opening for Kozuka in tsuba)

MEI 銘 (signatures)

MUMEI 無銘 (no signature)

MIMI 耳 (rim on a tsuba)

MOKKO-GATA 木瓜形 (four lobed shape)

MON (crest or symbol)

NAKAGO-ANA 中心穴 (opening in a tsuba through which the tang of the sword is fitted)

NAMI (wave)

NANAKO (raised dots on a flat base, lit'fish roe')

NANBAN (southern barbarian, foreign influenced design)

NIKU (raised border around & highlighting an opening)

OMOTE (表) (オモテ) (the front side)

SEKIGANE 責金 (metal filling in nakago-ana)

SHINCHI-ZOGAN (brass inlay)

TEGANE-ATO 鏨跡 (punch marks around the nakago-ana to tighten fit)

TEN-ZOGAN (dot inlay)

TSUCHIME-JI (hammered finish)

UDE-NUKI-ANA 腕貫穴 (two small holes in the Hira of some tsuba for attachment of a cord)

UME 埋 (a metal plug in the Kozuka and/or Kogai-ana.) (also Ategane)

URA 裏面 (the back side / reverse side)

WAKIZASHI 脇差 (smaller of the two swords usually worn by Samurai)

YAMAGATA (lit. mountain shape) (a hitsu-ana in this shape)

TEGANE-ATO 鏨跡 (punch marks around the nakago-ana to tighten fit of blade)

YO-SUKASHI (positive silhouette leaving only solid elements of the design)

ZOGAN 象嵌 (inlay)

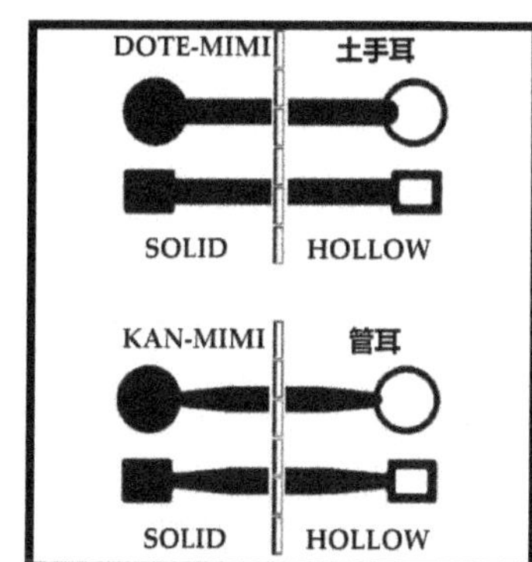

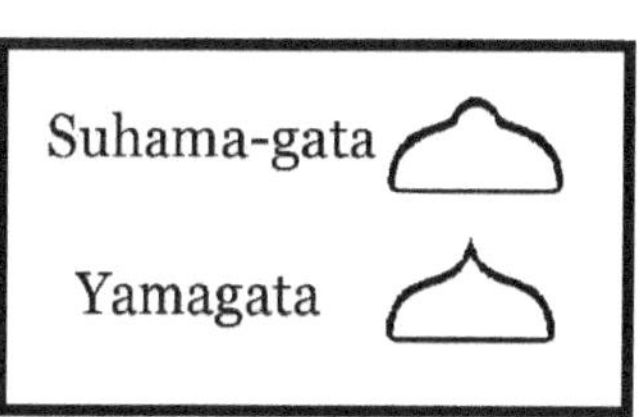

POSTCARDS

A series of fifty postcards depicting some of the most important schools and individual tsuba makers are reproduced here. A number have both the Omote and Ura views, with both Japanese descriptions and basic artists names and dates in English.

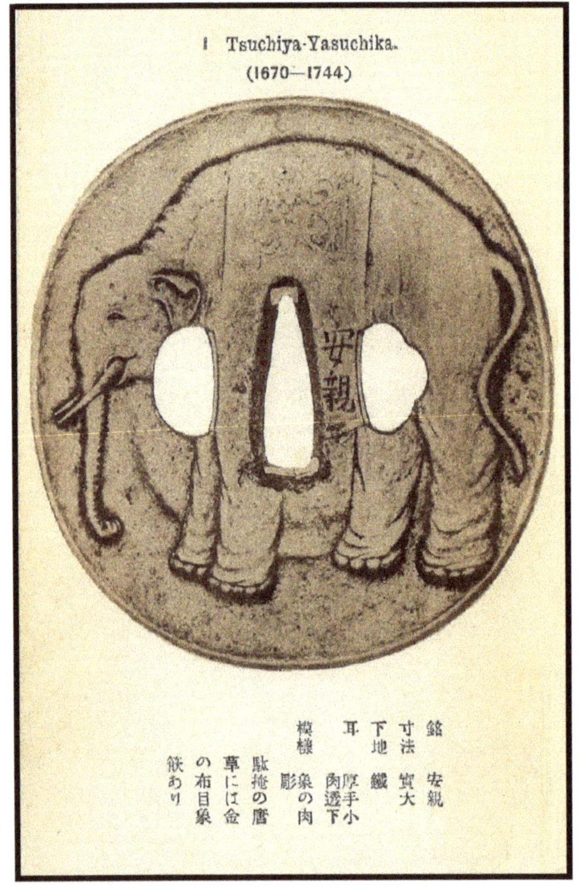

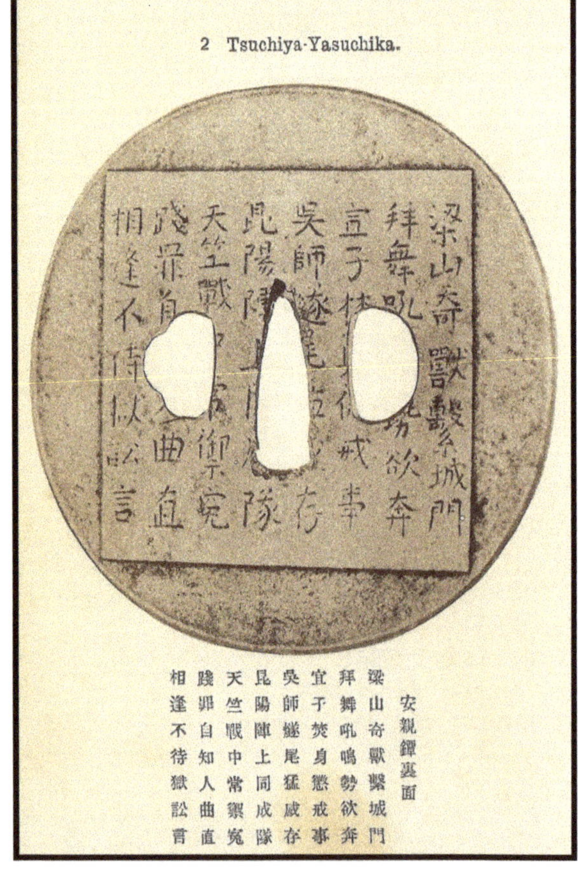

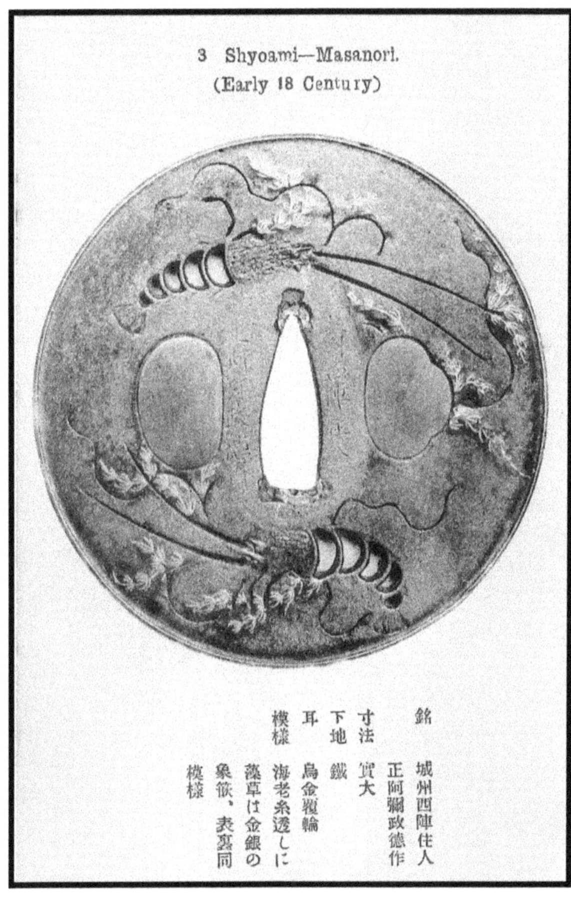

3　Shyoami—Masanori.
(Early 18 Century)

銘　　城州西陣住人
　　　正阿彌政德作
寸法　實大
下地　鐵
耳　　烏金覆輪
模様　海老糸透しに
　　　藻草は金銀の
　　　象嵌、表裏同
　　　模様

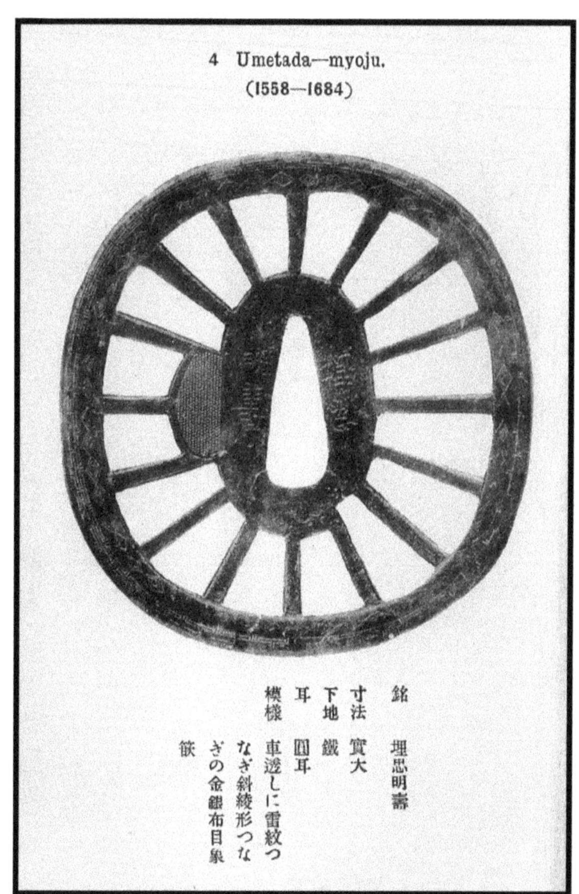

4　Umetada—myoju.
(1558—1684)

銘　　埋忠明壽
寸法　實大
下地　鐵
耳　　圓耳
模様　車透しに雷紋つ
　　　なぎ斜綾形つ
　　　ぎの金銀布目象
　　　嵌

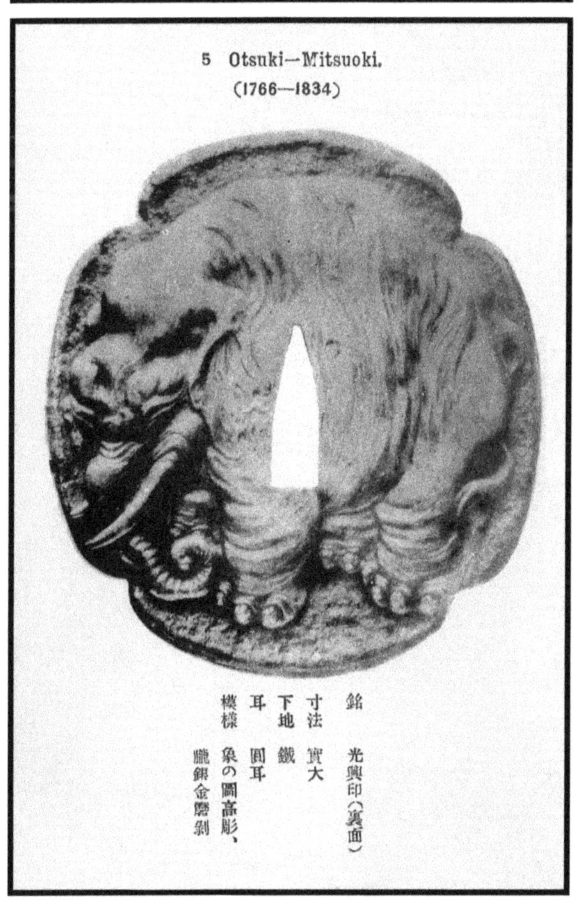

5　Otsuki—Mitsuoki.
(1766—1834)

銘　　光興印（裏面）
寸法　實大
下地　鐵
耳　　圓耳
模様　象の圖高彫、
　　　朧銀金罍剝

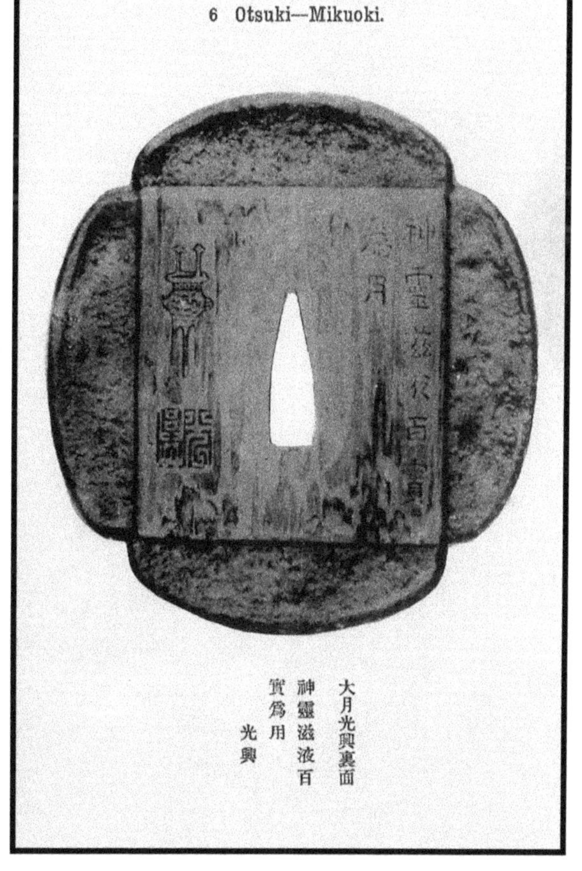

6　Otsuki—Mikuoki.

銘　　大月光興裏面
　　　神靈滋波百
實爲用
光興

7 Shyoami·Chiknyu.
(End 16 Century)

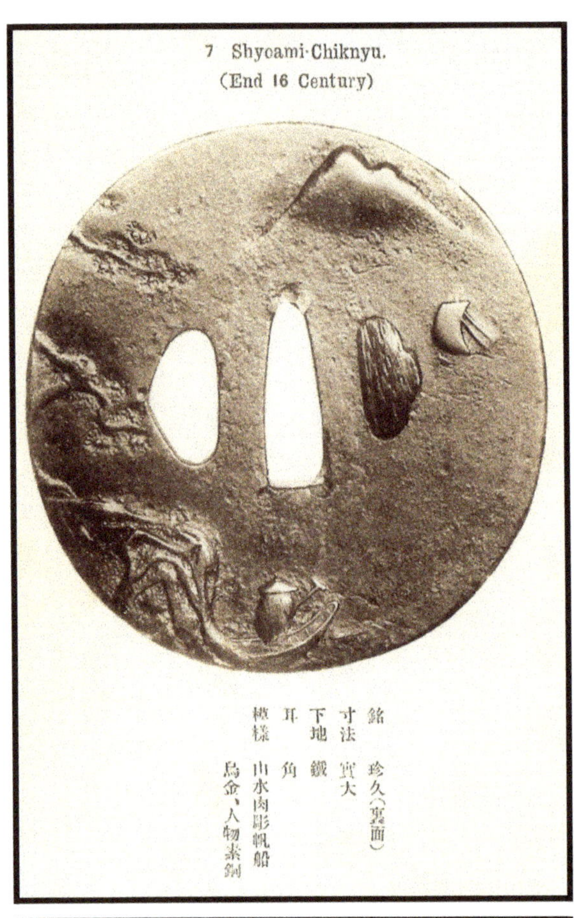

銘　珍久（裏面）
寸法　實大
下地　鐡
耳　角
模様　山水肉彫帆船
　　　烏金、人物素銅

8 Shyoami·Chiknyu.

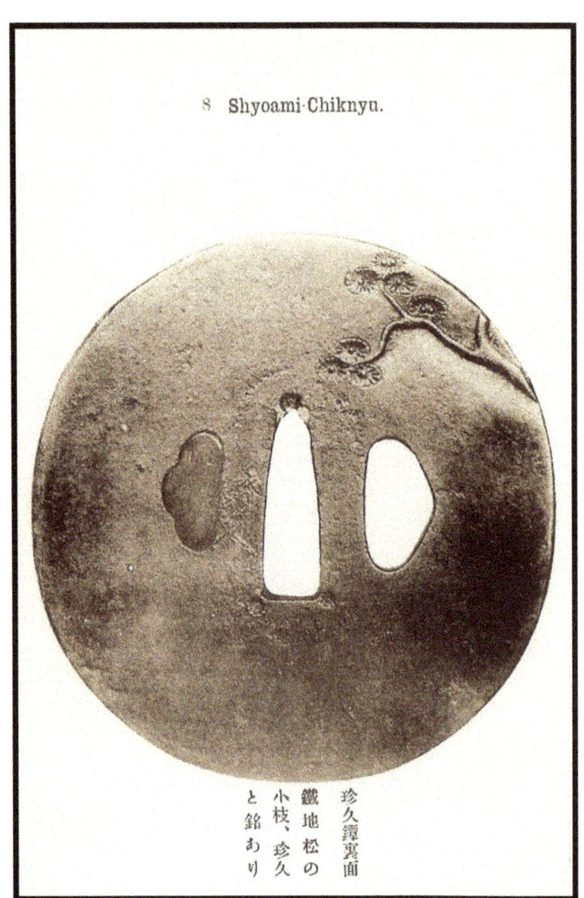

珍久鐔裏面
鐡地松の
小枝、珍久
と銘あり

9
Koike—
Yoohiro.
（End. 16
Century）

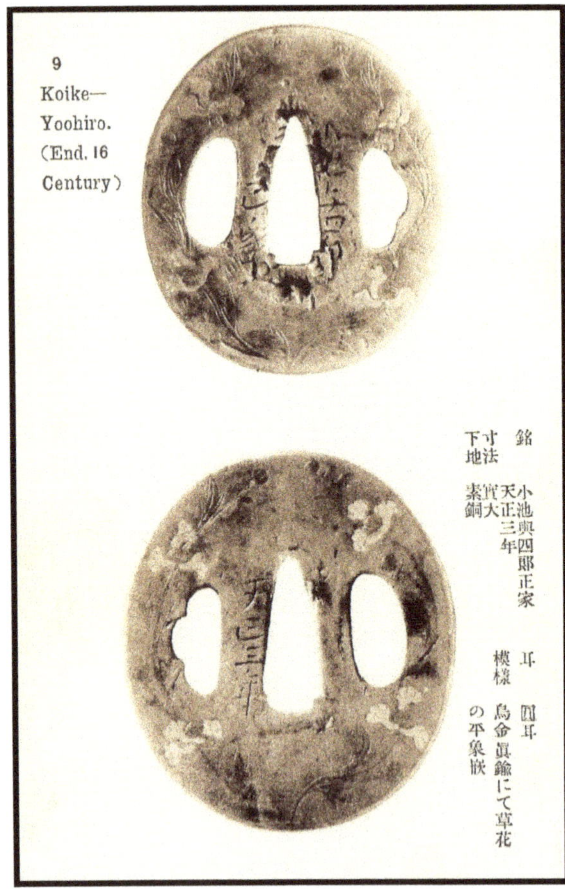

銘　小池與四郎正家　天正三年
寸法　實大
下地　素銅
耳　四耳
模様　烏金眞鍮にて草花の平象嵌

10 Old Heianjo.
(Middle 15 Century)

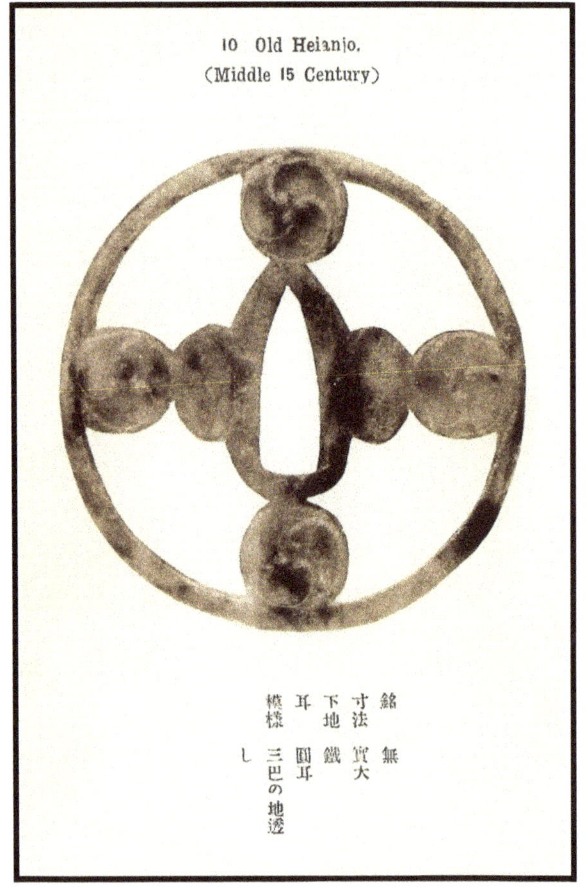

銘　無
寸法　實大
下地　鐡
耳　圓耳
模様　三巴の地透し

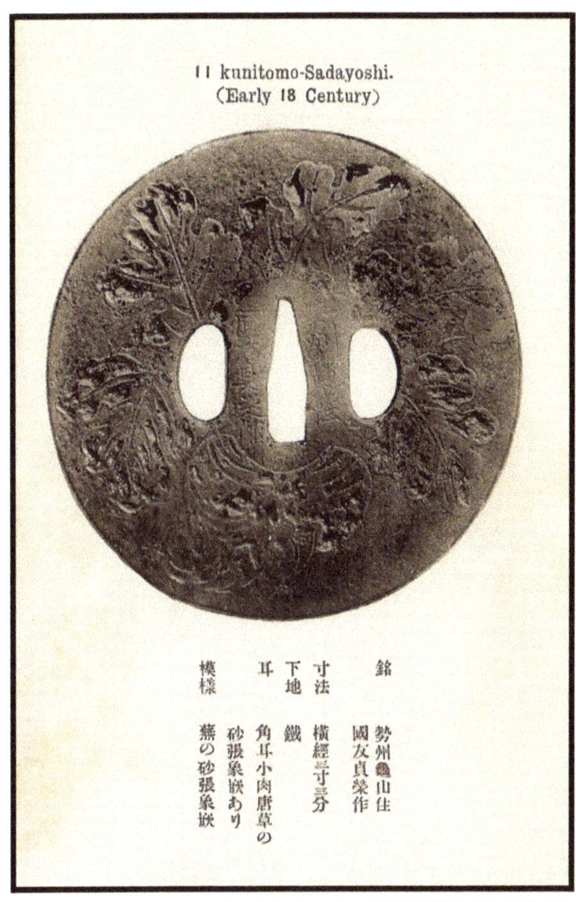

11 kunitomo-Sadayoshi.
(Early 18 Century)

銘　　勢州[印]山住
　　　國友貞榮作
寸法　横經寸三分
下地　鐵
耳　　角耳小肉唐草の
　　　砂張象嵌あり
模様　蕨の砂張象嵌

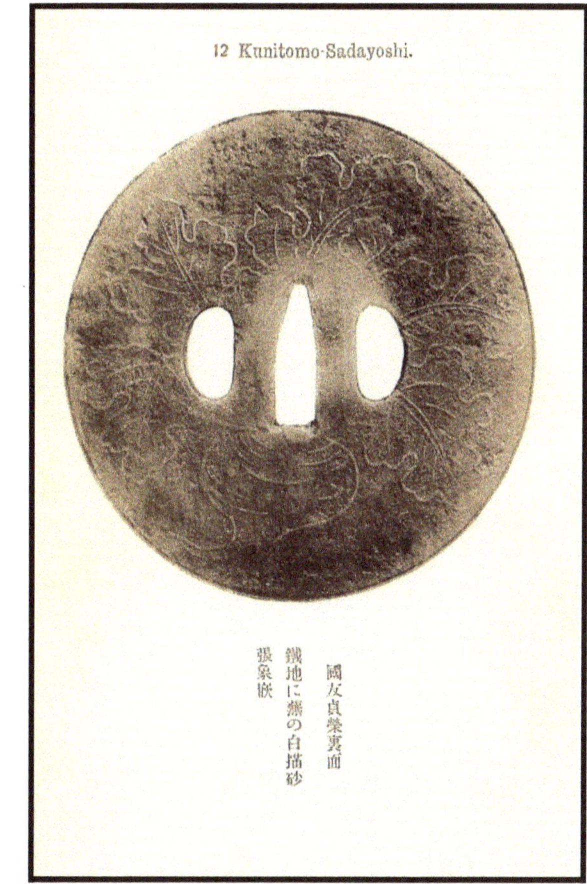

12 Kunitomo-Sadayoshi.

國友貞榮裏面
鐵地に蕨の白描砂
張象嵌

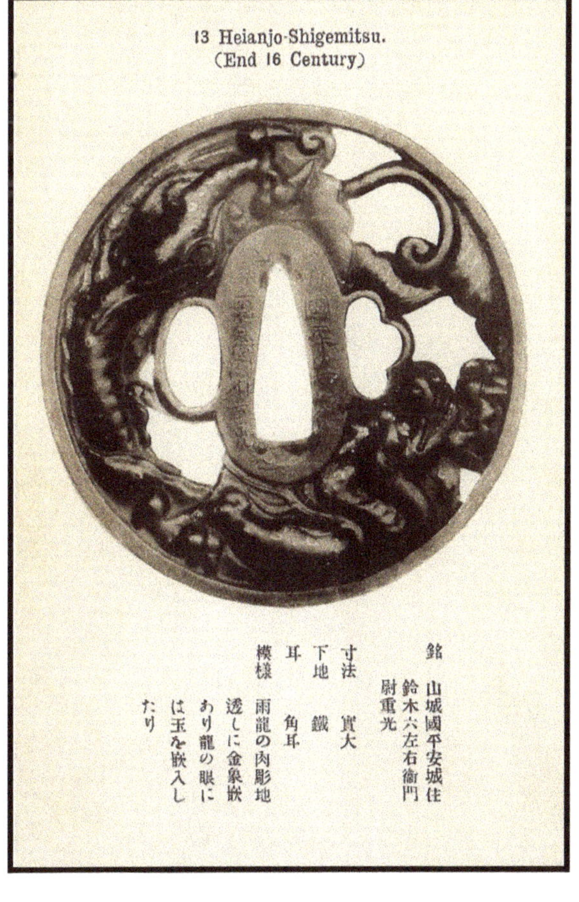

13 Heianjo-Shigemitsu.
(End 16 Century)

銘　　山城國平安城住
　　　鈴木六左右衛門
　　　尉重光
寸法　實大
下地　鐵
耳　　角耳
模様　雨龍の肉彫地
　　　透しに金象嵌
　　　あり龍の眼に
　　　は玉を嵌入し
　　　たり

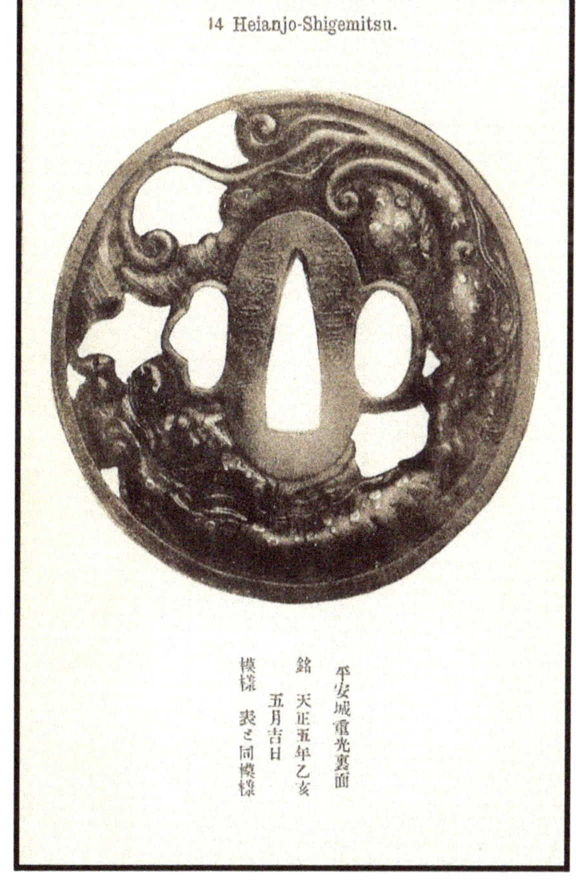

14 Heianjo-Shigemitsu.

銘　　平安城重光裏面
　　　天正五年乙亥
　　　五月吉日
模様　表と同模様

銘　　無

寸法　實大

下地　鐵

耳　　角耳小肉

模樣　桐の陰陽地透し

銘　　宣花押

寸法　實大

下地　四分一

耳　　角耳

模樣　雲形の透しに
　　　烏金地の虎符
　　　形に金銀色繪
　　　の虎ミ文字の
　　　据紋象嵌

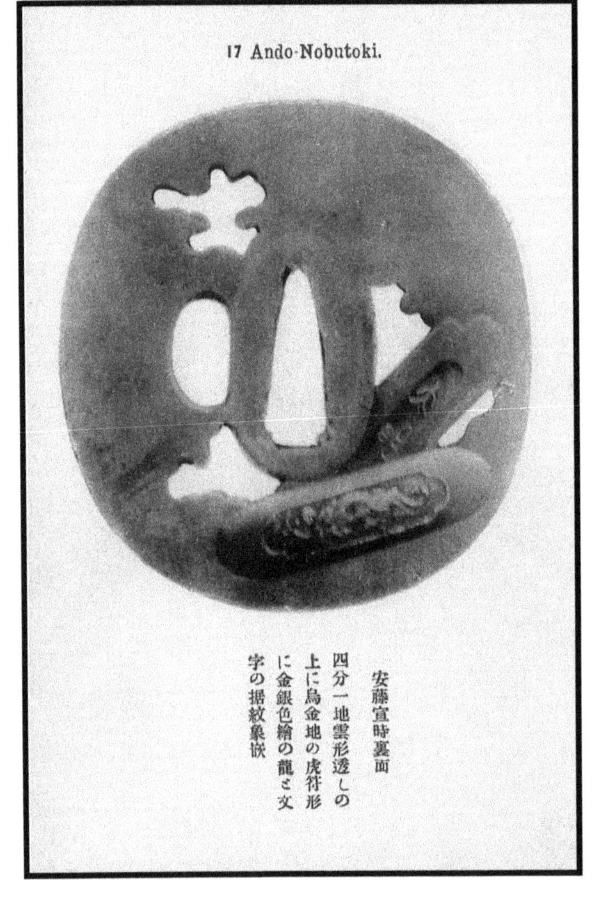

安藤宣時裏面
四分一地雲形透しの
上に烏金地の虎符形
に金銀色繪の龍ミ文
字の据紋象嵌

銘　　無

寸法　實大

下地　鐵

耳　　圓耳

模樣　秋草の金布
　　　目象嵌

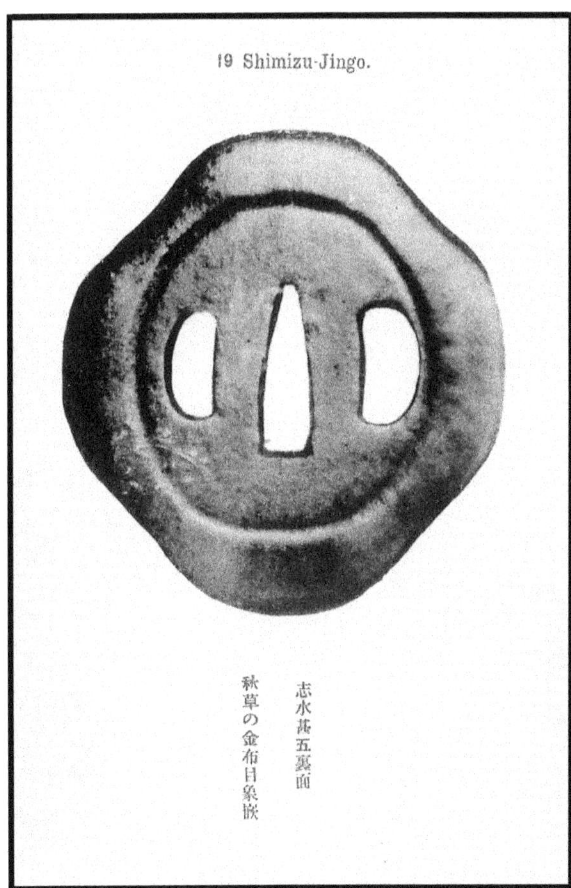

志水甚五裏面
秋草の金布目象嵌

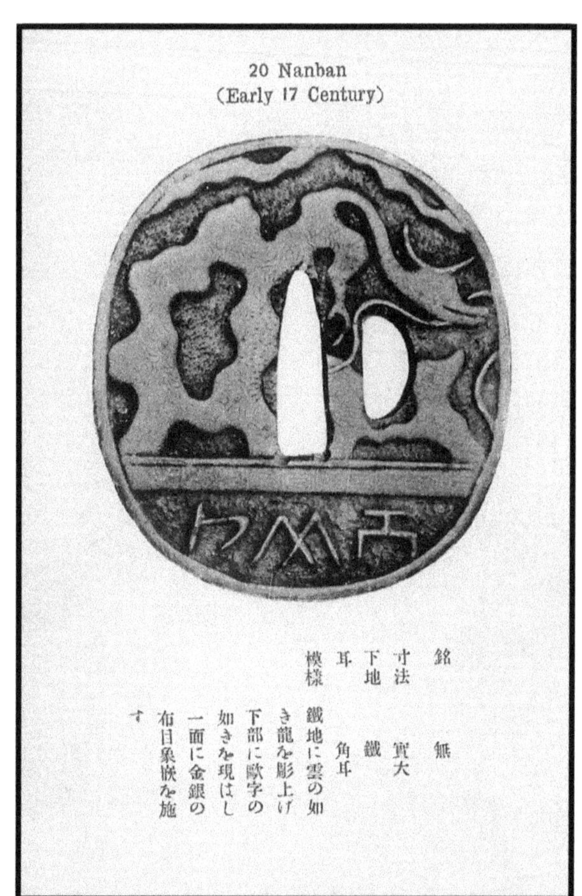

銘　無
寸法　實大
下地　鐵
耳　角耳
模樣　鐵地に雲の如き龍を彫上げ下部に歐字の如きを現はし一面に金銀の布目象嵌を施す

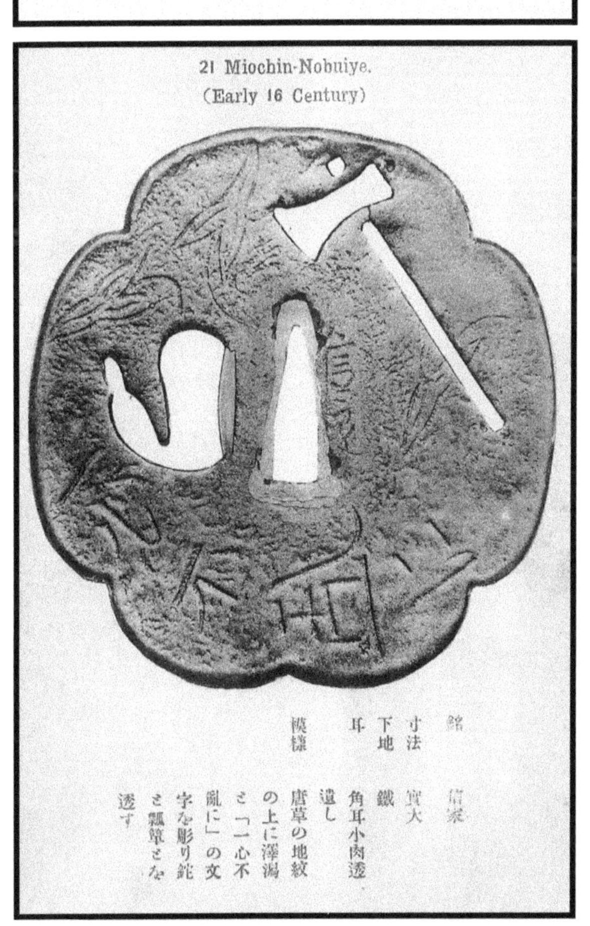

銘　信家
寸法　實大
下地　鐵
耳　角耳小肉透遶し
模樣　唐草の地紋の上に澤潟さ「一心不亂に「」の字を彫り鈍さ瓢草さな透す

信家裏面
唐草模樣の地紋の上に澤潟と涙を彫り鈍さ瓢草さな透す

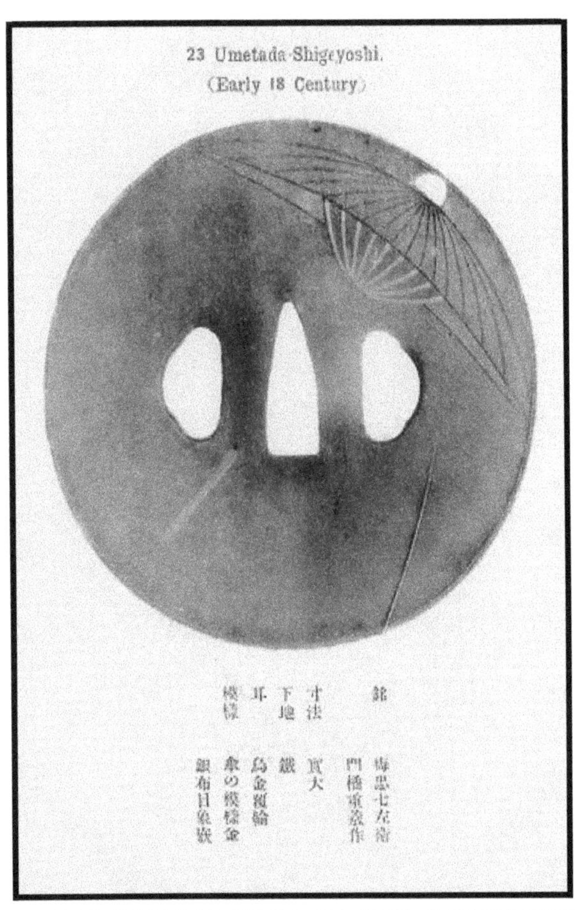

23 Umetada-Shigeyoshi.
(Early 18 Century)

銘　梅忠七左衛門橘重嘉作
寸法　實大
下地　鐵
耳　烏金覆輪
模樣　傘の模樣金銀布目象嵌

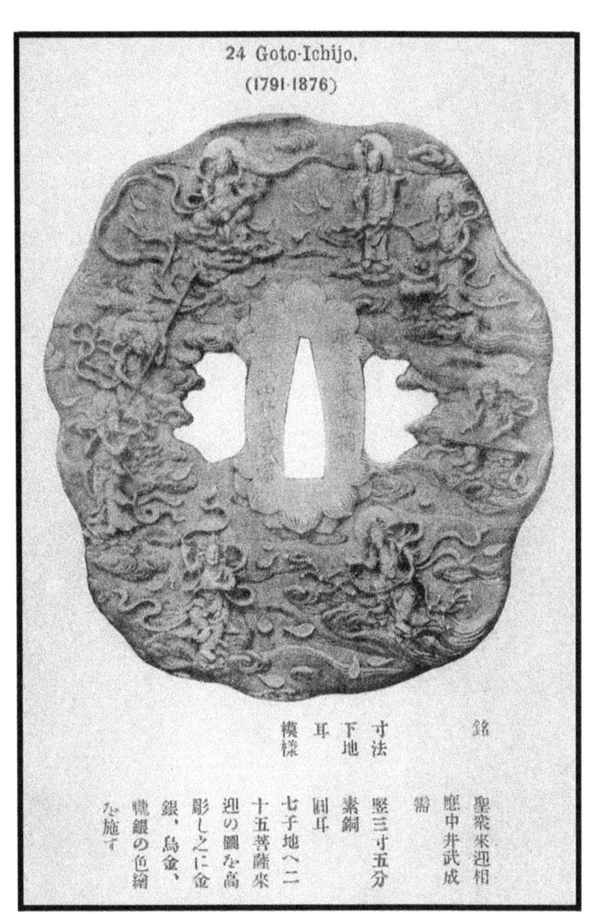

24 Goto-Ichijo.
(1791-1876)

銘　聖衆來迎相　應中井武成　需
寸法　竪三寸五分
下地　素銅
耳　圓耳
模樣　七子地へ二十五菩薩來迎の圖な高彫し之に金銀、烏金、朧銀の色繪を施す

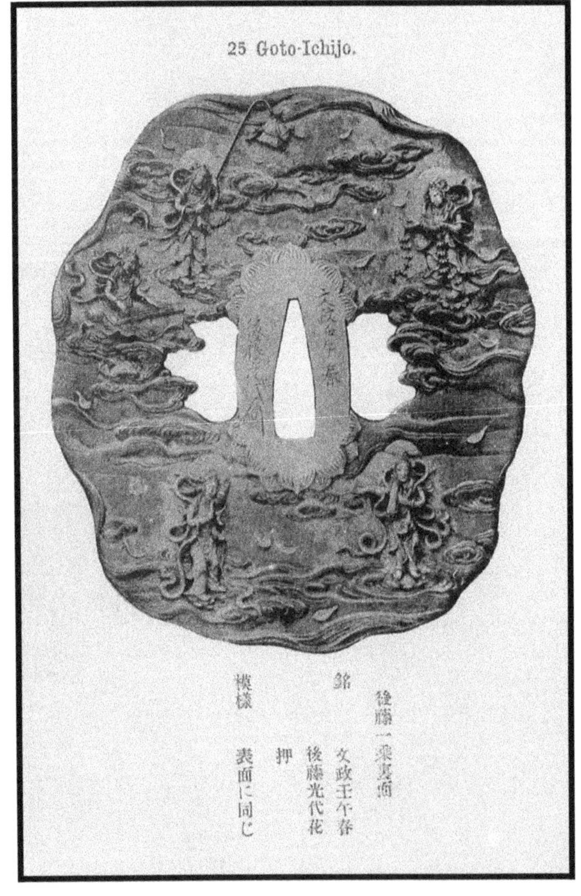

25 Goto-Ichijo.

銘　後藤一乗真面　文政壬午春　後藤光代花　押
模樣　表面に同じ

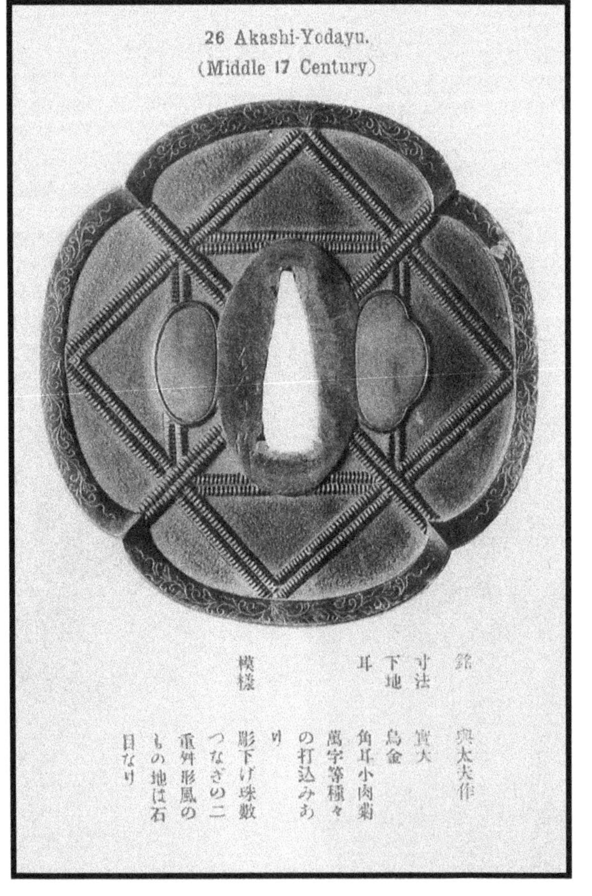

26 Akashi-Yodayu.
(Middle 17 Century)

銘　奥太夫作
寸法　實大
下地　烏金
耳　角耳小肉菊萬字等種々の打込みあり
模樣　影下げ珠数つなぎの二重舞形風のもの地は石目なり

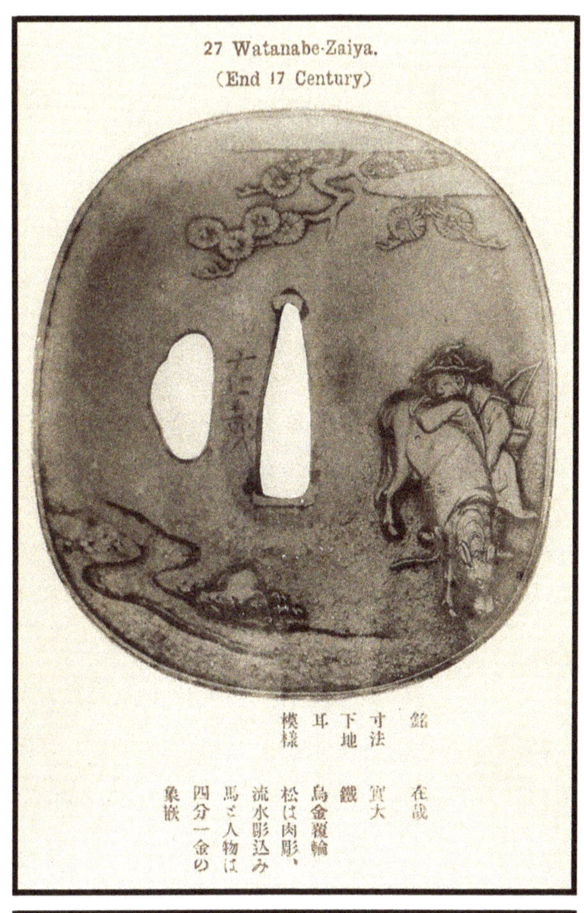

27 Watanabe-Zaiya.
(End 17 Century)

銘　在哉
寸法　寅大
下地　鐵
耳　烏金覆輪
模様　松は肉彫、流水彫込み、馬ご人物は四分一金の象嵌

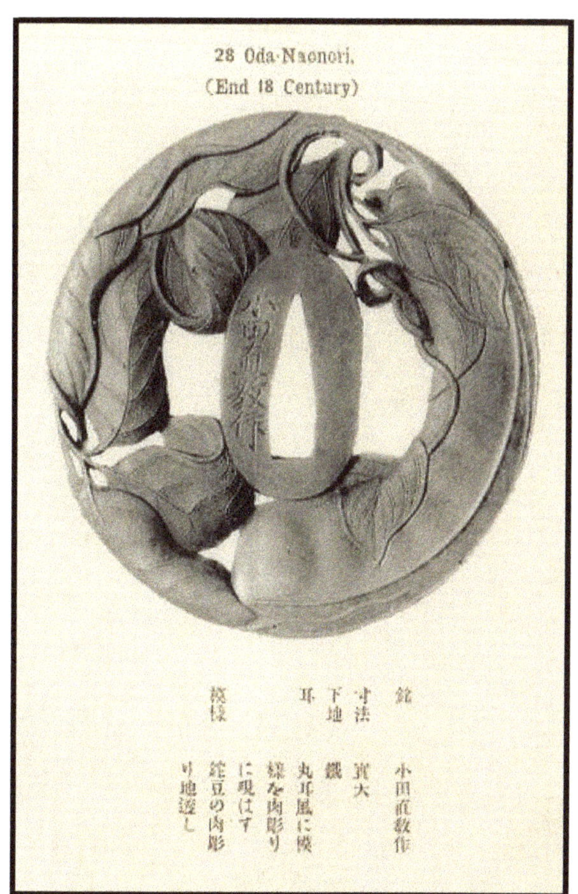

28 Oda-Naonori.
(End 18 Century)

銘　小田直教作
寸法　寅大
下地　鐵
耳　丸耳風に模様を肉彫りに現はす
模様　莢豆の肉彫り地透し

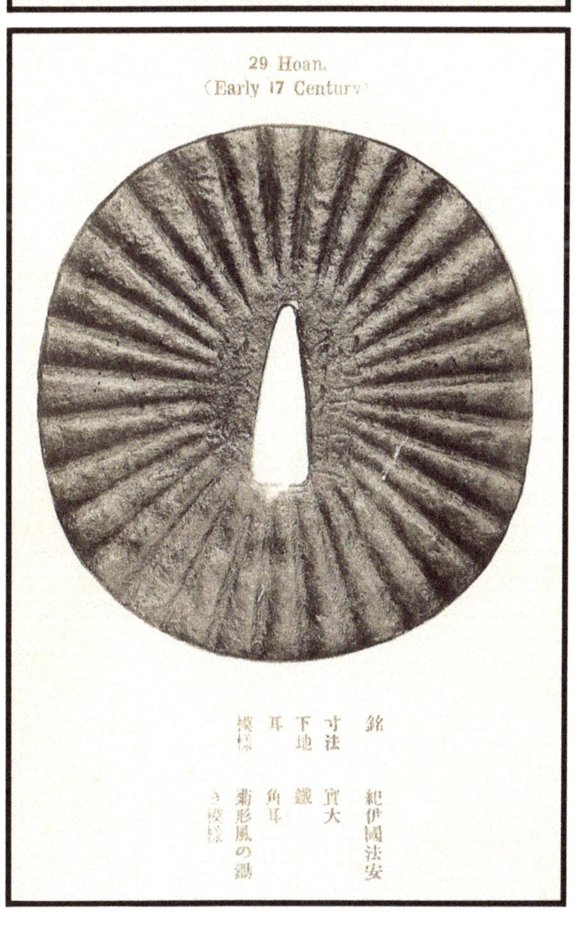

29 Hoan.
(Early 17 Century)

銘　紀伊國法安
寸法　寅大
下地　鐵
耳　角耳
模様　菊形風の鍔の模様

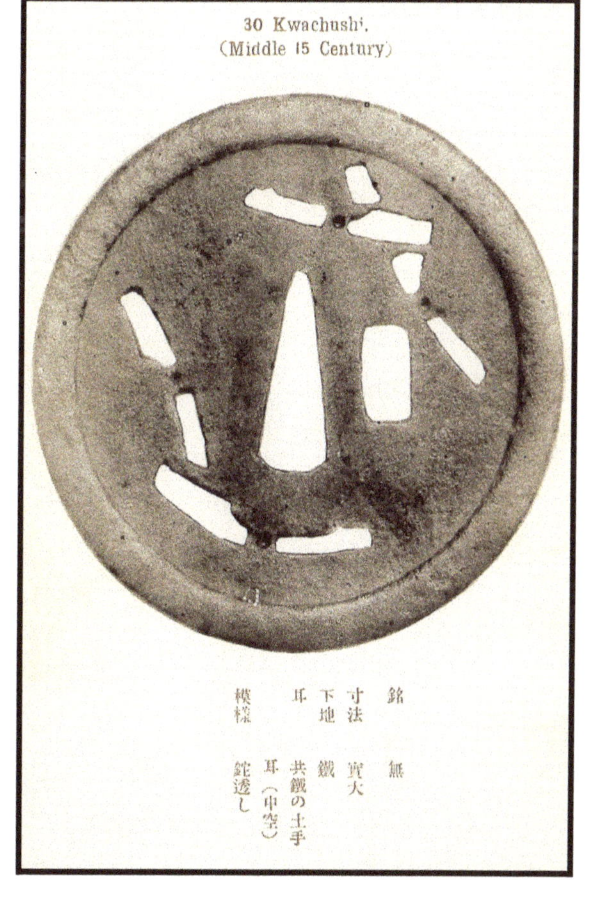

30 Kwachushi.
(Middle 15 Century)

銘　無
寸法　寅大
下地　鐵
耳　共鐵の土手耳（中空）
模様　鋲透し

31 Old Shoami.
(Middle 16 Century)

銘　無
寸法　横徑二寸九分五厘
下地　鐵
耳　四耳
模樣　唐草の金象嵌

33 Nara-Toshinaga.
(1667-1736)

銘　利壽　裏に金象嵌
寸法　寅大
下地　鐵
耳　角頻ろ厚し
模樣　大森彦七鬼　女の肉彫金　銀烏金の象嵌

32 Kaneie.
(Middle 15 Century)

銘　堀州伏見住　金家
寸法　寅大
下地　鐵
耳　打返し
模樣　大袋せる波　闇の半身像　前齒二個は　金象嵌なり

34 Nara-Toshinaga.

利壽裏面
銘　利壽花押金象嵌
模樣　表より續ける模　樣右に樹木な肉　彫したり

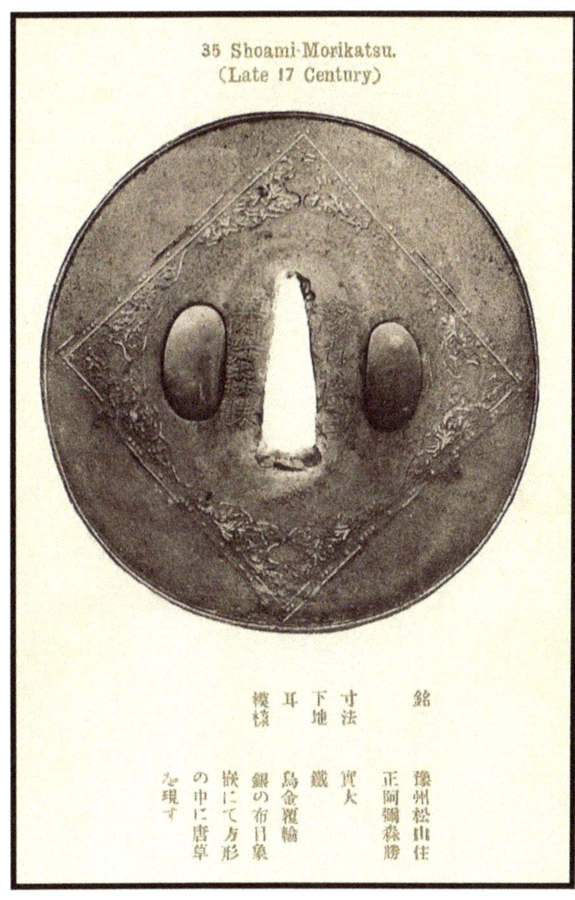

35 Shoami-Morikatsu.
(Late 17 Century)

銘　豫州松山住　正阿彌森勝
寸法　實大
下地　鐵
耳　烏金覆輪
模樣　銀の布目象嵌にて方形の中に唐草を現す

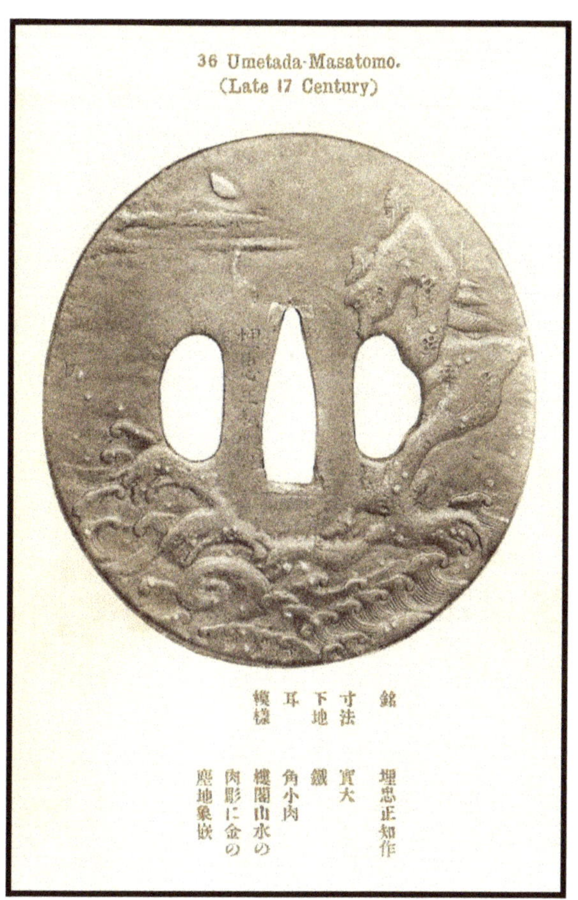

36 Umetada-Masatomo.
(Late 17 Century)

銘　埋忠正知作
寸法　實大
下地　鐵
耳　角小肉
模樣　樓閣山水の肉彫に金の庭地象嵌

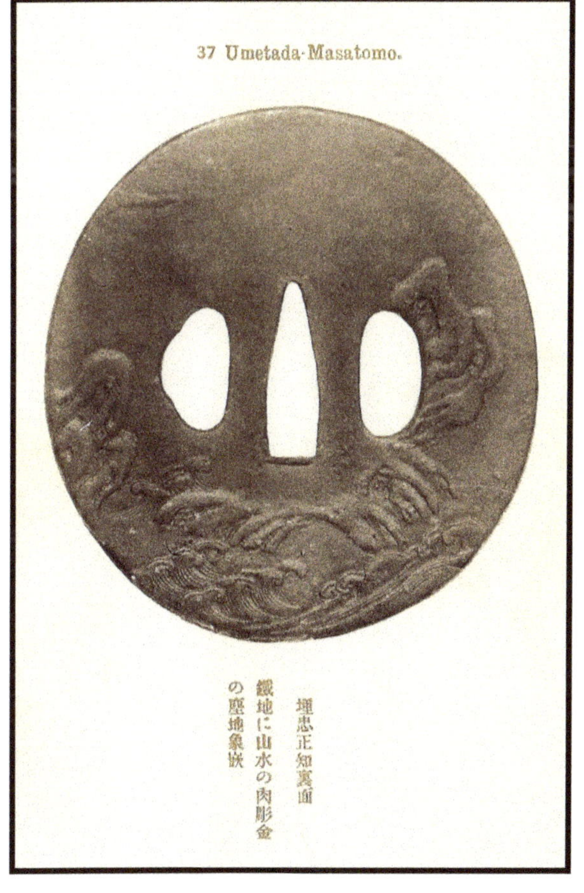

37 Umetada-Masatomo.

埋忠正知裏面
鐵地に山水の肉彫金の庭地象嵌

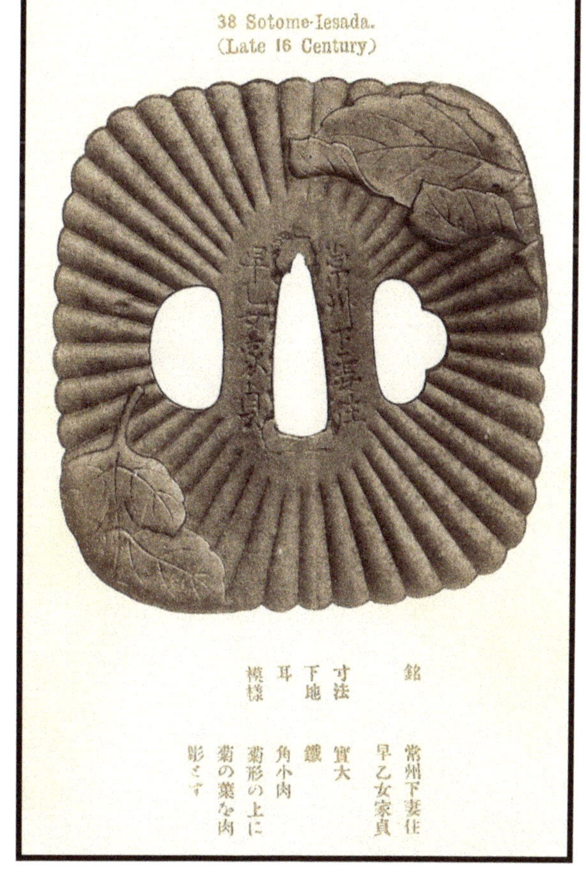

38 Sotome-Iesada.
(Late 16 Century)

銘　常州下妻住　早乙女家貞
寸法　實大
下地　鐵
耳　角小肉
模樣　菊形の上に菊の葉な肉彫とす

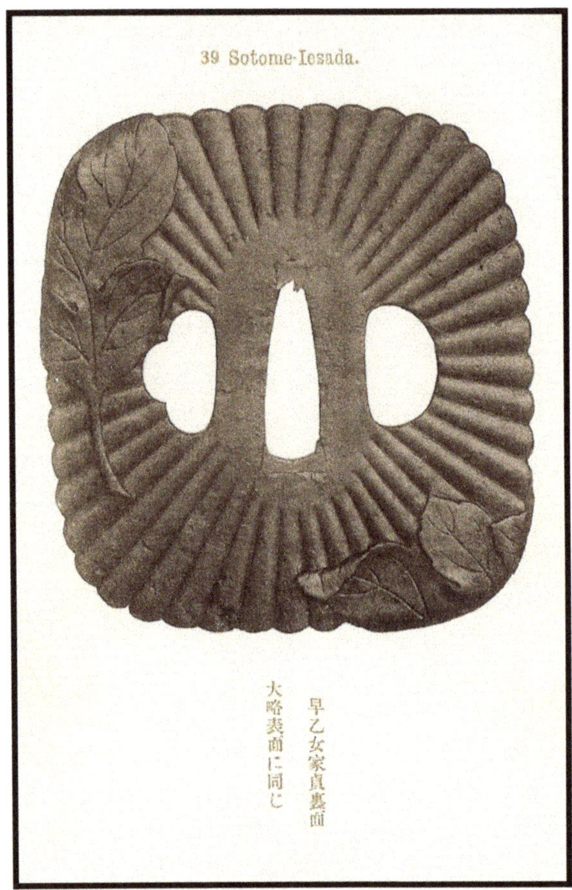

39 Sotome-Iesada.

早乙女家貞裏面
大略表面に同じ

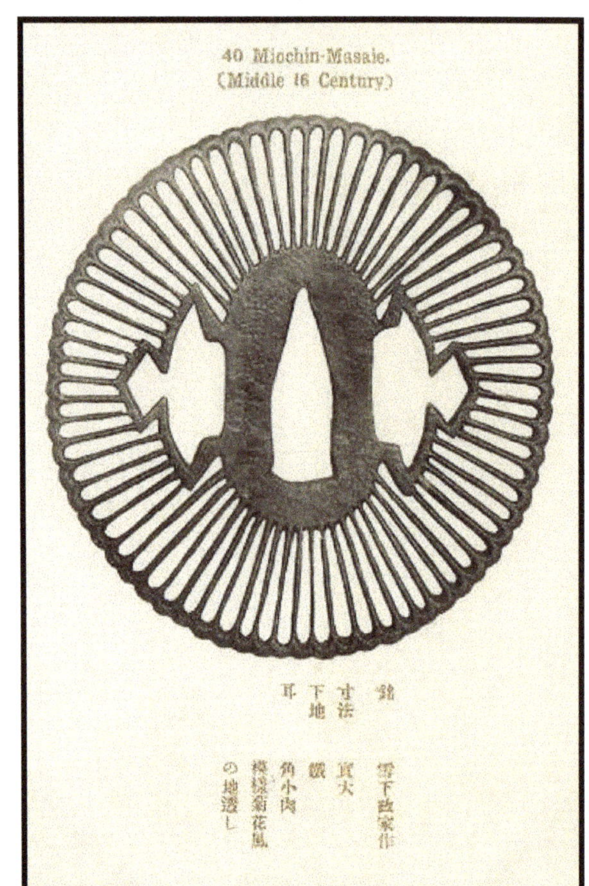

40 Miochin-Masaie.
(Middle 16 Century)

銘　雪下政家作
寸法　實大
下地　鐵
耳　角小肉
模様菊花風
の地透し

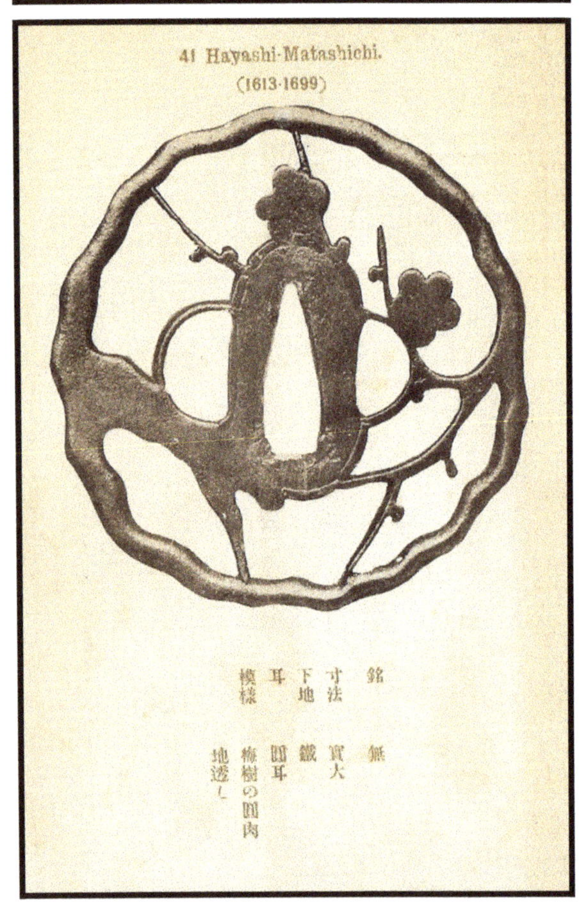

41 Hayashi-Matashichi.
(1613-1699)

銘　無
寸法　實大
下地　鐵
耳　圓耳
模様　梅樹の圓肉
地透し

42 Ichinomiya-Nagatsune.
(1722-1786)

銘　長常花押
寸法　實大
下地　四分一
耳　角
模様　人物に馬を
肉影しに
金、銀、烏金
素銅を象嵌
す

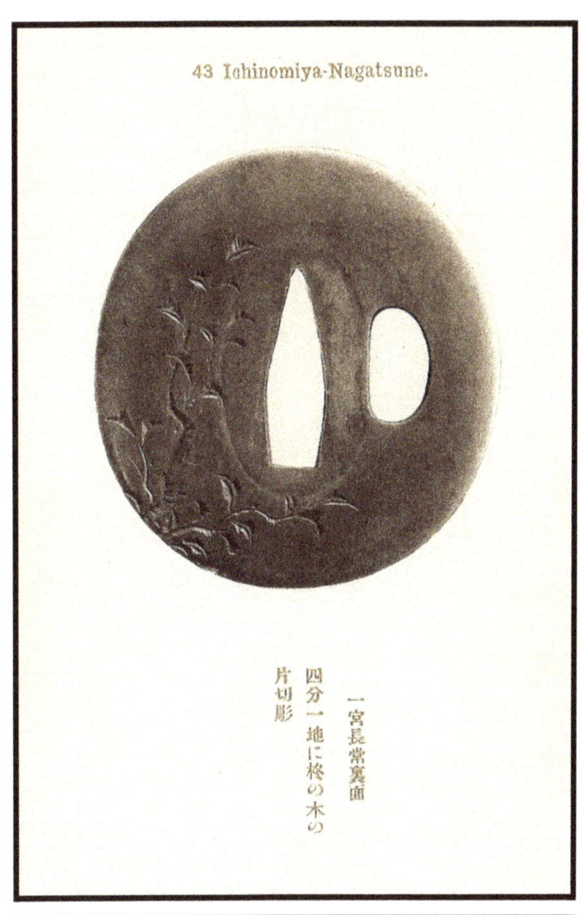

一宮長常裏面
四分一地に柊の木の
片切彫

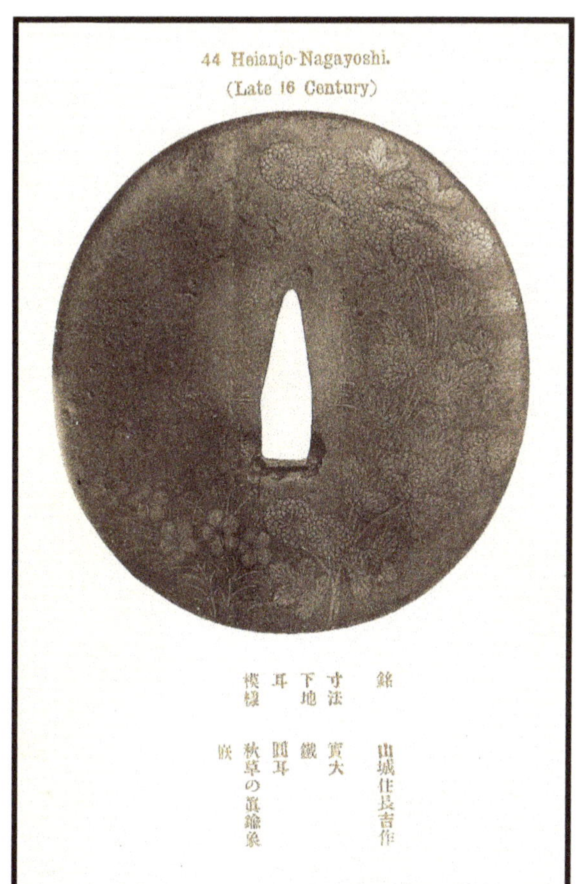

銘　　山城住長吉作
寸法　　尺大
下地　　鐵
耳　　圓耳
模樣　　秋草の眞鍮象
　　　嵌

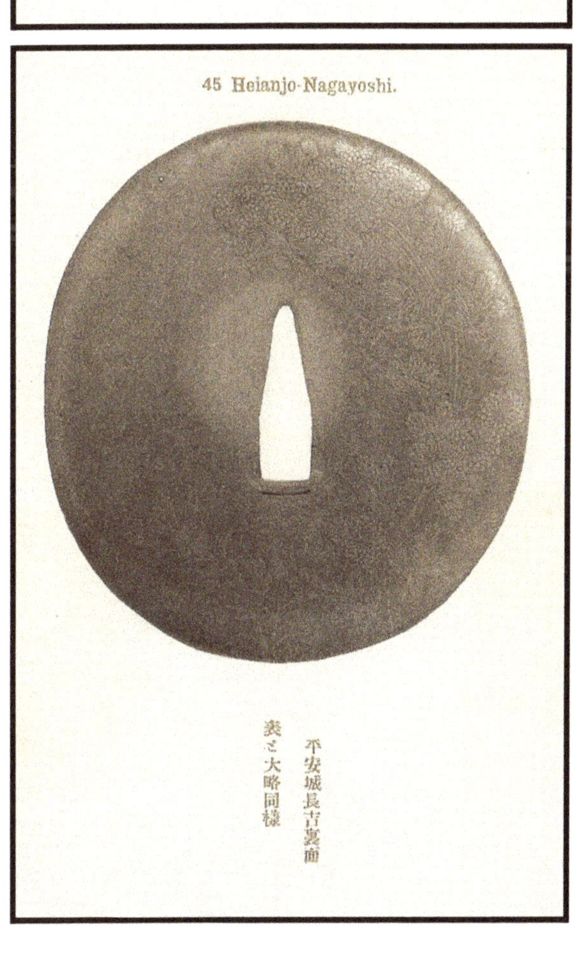

平安城長吉裏面
裏さ大略同様

銘　　源可法
寸法　　橫徑三寸
下地　　鐵
耳　　圓耳
模樣　　耳に近く白
　　　銀布目象嵌
　　　にて模様風
　　　の輪郭を取
　　　り「馬到成
　　　功」の文字
　　　を同じ布目
　　　象嵌にて現
　　　す

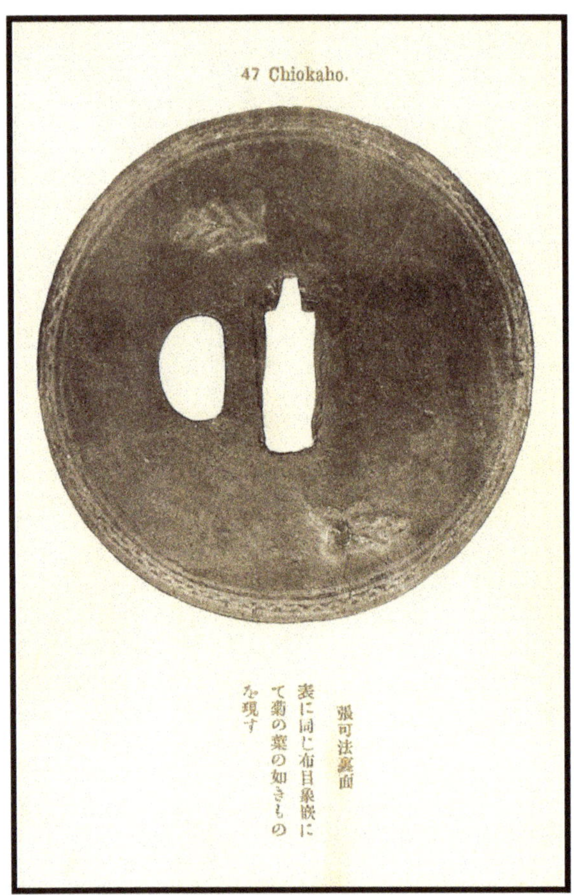

47 Chiokaho.

張可法裏面
表に同じ布目象嵌に
て菊の葉の如きもの
を現す

48 Akasaka-Tadamasa.
（―1657）

銘　無
寸法　實大
下地　鐵
耳　圓耳
模樣　竹に丁子と
　　　船を地透し
　　　す

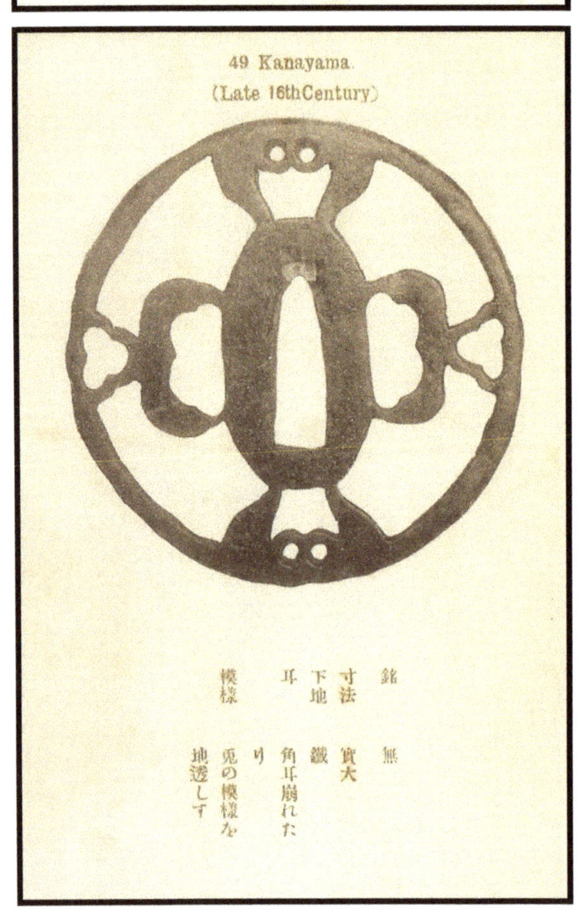

49 Kanayama.
(Late 16thCentury)

銘　無
寸法　實大
下地　鐵
耳　角耳崩れた
　　　り
模樣　兎の模樣を
　　　地透しす

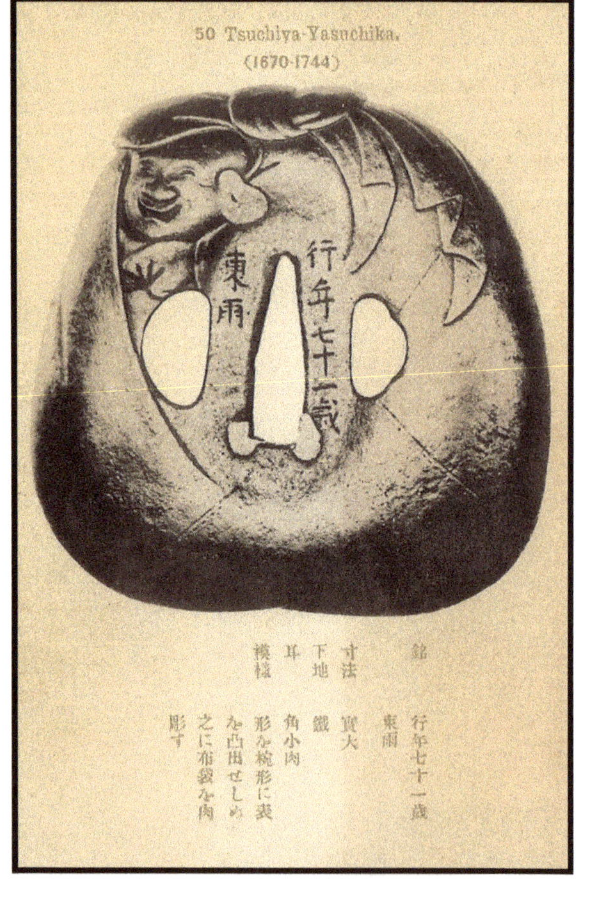

50 Tsuchiya-Yasuchika.
（1670-1744）

銘　東雨
　　行年七十一歳
寸法　實大
下地　鐵
耳　角小肉
模樣　形を椀形に表
　　　を凸出せしめ
　　　之に布袋を肉
　　　彫す

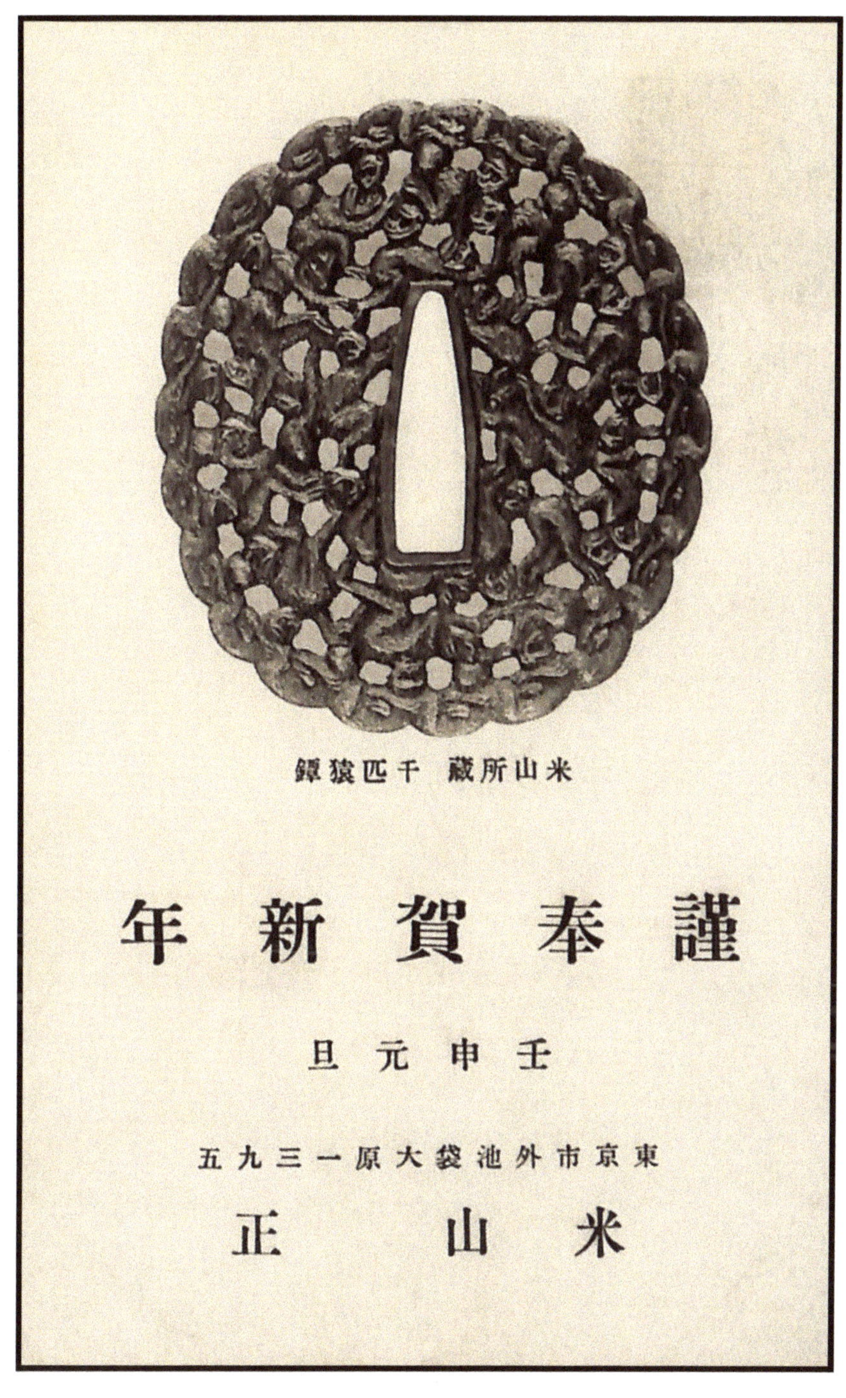

'Happy New Year' postcard featuring the theme of the "Thousand Monkeys"
This card is not part of the series of fifty.